Usborne

Write Your Own Family History

Ideas by

Jane Bingham

Design by

Stephanie Jeffries

Illustrations by

Ro Ledesma, Giovana Medeiros and Anna Simeone

Edited by

Felicity Brooks

Expert advice from

Rebecca Brooks at Adoption UK

And words and pictures by YOU!

This is the family history of

____

Write your name here.

Contents

Looking at families

Getting started

First memories and growing up

Usborne

Write Your Own Family History

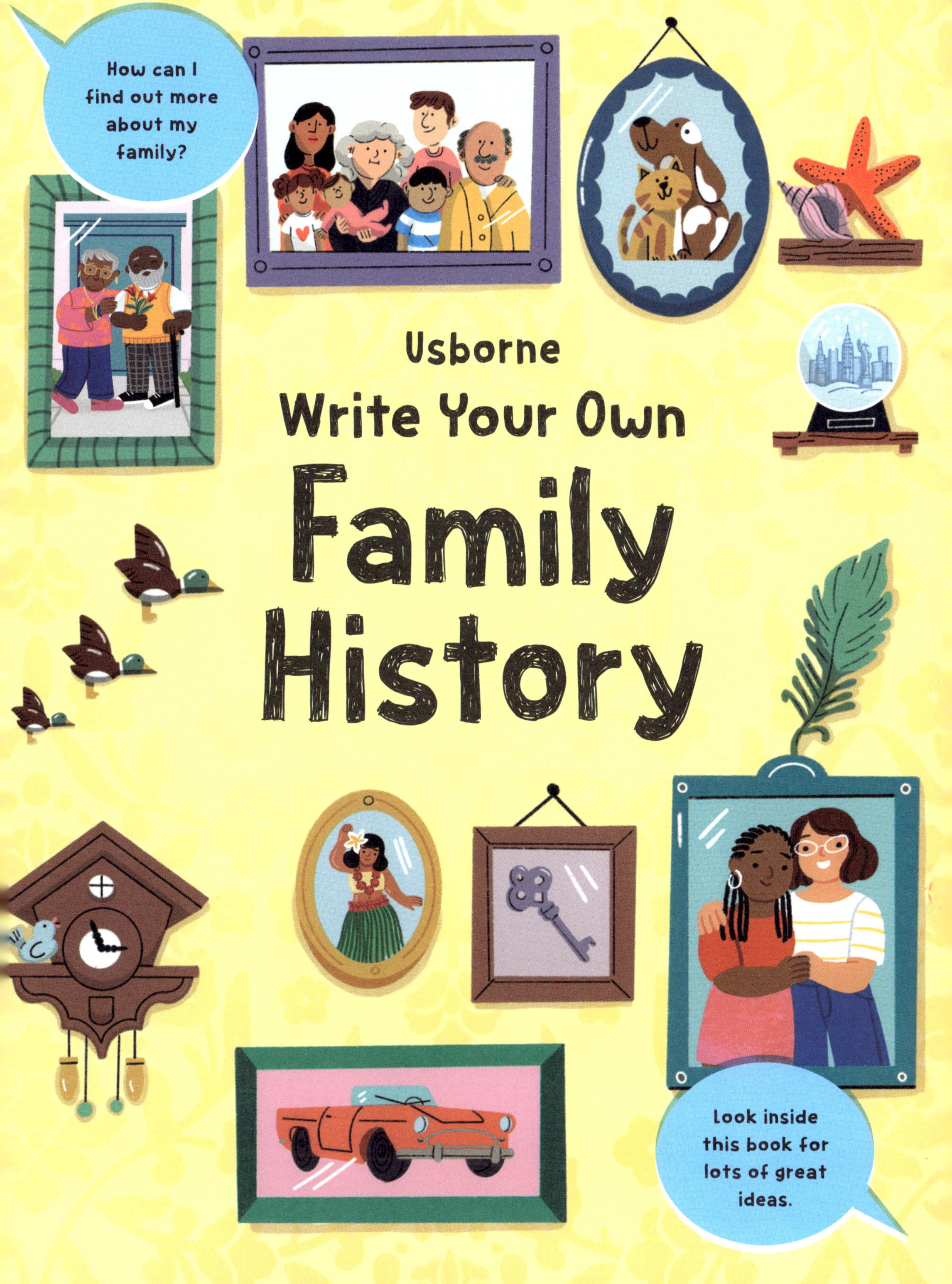

Stick a photo of your family here.

This is my family.

Family history is for EVERYONE

All families are different – and each family has its own stories.

Children may live with their birth parents, step-parents, adoptive parents or foster parents.* Some live with relatives or with guardians – caring adults who look after them.

All these special grown-ups are part of a family group and they all have stories to tell.

Whatever kind of family group you belong to, this book is for YOU!

*Look at the list on page 94 if you're not sure what some of these words mean.

Work, leisure and sport

Life at home

Travel and holidays

Living through history

Telling your family story

You can use this page for anything you like.

Looking at families

What makes a family?

This section takes a look at families of all kinds. You'll find pages to fill in on you and your family, and a space to create your own family gallery.

All about me

At the heart of your family is someone you know very well. Make a start on your family story by filling in these pages all about YOU.

Age:

Name:

Add a photo or drawing of yourself here.

Five good things about me...

1

2

3

4

5

Some drawings of things I like

My friends – and why I like them:

My superpower would be...

Me as a superhero

My favourite things to do:

When I grow up, I would like to be...

What makes a family?

Your family is made up of you and the people who care for you. There may be just one person looking after you, or there may be many. No two families are exactly the same.

We are family!

Some family groups include close friends or neighbours. And pets can be important family members too.

Who do I live with?

Use this space for photos, drawings and the names of the people you live with.

More about families

Families are made up of people who belong to different age groups, known as 'generations'. Children, parents and grandparents each belong to a different generation.

Having older generations in your family makes life extra interesting. Even if you don't have grandparents of your own, you may know some older people who you can talk to.

Here are three generations of one family: the children, their parents, and their grandparents.

Me and my sister

Mum and Dad

Grandma and Grandpa

Past generations

This is my great-great-great grandma. She lived five generations before me!

Some people know a lot about their family's history. They can trace their family members back through many generations.

Jane Reynolds, 1890

More family members

Families often include children, parents and grandparents, but there are many other kinds of family members. Do you have any of these people in your family?

✓ I have a...

- ○ half-sibling
- ○ step-sibling
- ○ step-parent
- ○ aunt
- ○ uncle
- ○ cousin
- ○ great aunt
- ○ great uncle

Some children have adoptive parents, foster parents or guardians – special grown-ups who look after them. They are all important family members.

My family gallery

This empty gallery is waiting to be filled with your family. Aim to show several generations, if you can. You might also like to show some family friends and pets.

Fill these frames with photos or drawings.

Use these spaces to write the names of your family members and their relationship to you.

This frame is reserved for YOU!

Looking at your gallery, which family members might you be able to interview for your family history?

Mark the ones you've chosen with a star. *

Do you already know some stories about your grown-ups' lives? You could write them here.

Getting started

How do you find out about your family history?

This section has helpful tips on asking questions, looking at photos and objects, and getting ready to research.

What is family history?

What do you think of when you see the words 'family history'?

Maybe you see a pile of ancient documents...

...some portraits of ancestors...

...and a family tree stretching back over time?

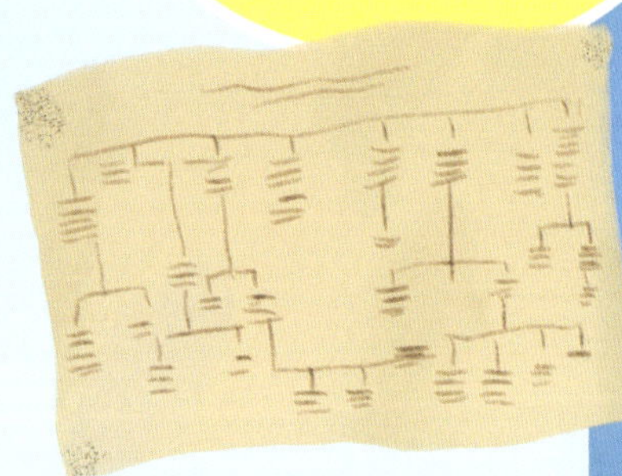

Research into the distant past can be fascinating, but family history is <u>much more than that</u>. It's about discovering your family stories NOW.

Our family history is made up of all our memories.

Once you start talking to people in your family, you'll find there's lots to discover...

✓ Ask about your grown-ups' early memories.

✓ Look at old photos together.

✓ Try finding out about treasured objects.

You may learn all kinds of things you never knew.

Building a story

As you find out more about your grown-ups' past, you can start to piece together your very own family history.

Looking at photos

You can learn a lot about the past by looking at old photos. Ask your grown-ups if they have some photographs to show you.

Many people have framed photos of special family moments.

Where are these children going?

Who is Great Granny taking for a walk?

Find out more

Ask about the people in the photos and try to find out when and where the pictures were taken.

Who is playing that strange musical instrument?

Why are they wearing such fancy clothes?

Does your family have any photo albums, or maybe an old box full of photos?

Looking at objects

Photos aren't the only evidence of the past. People often keep special things that help to tell their story.

Have I told you the tale of these broken glasses?

Your family may have kept...

Letters and postcards

School reports and exercise books

Holiday souvenirs

Medals and awards

Ask your grown-ups why they treasure these things.

Clothes and jewellery

I want you to have this locket. My great aunt gave it to me for my 16th birthday.

Asking questions

Learning about your family starts with asking questions, but first you need to decide...

Who would I like to talk to?

What would I like to find out?

Who to talk to?

Start with the people you see every day...

- Talk to your grown-ups about their memories.
- Ask about important moments in their lives.
- Don't forget to ask for ideas on who to talk to next.

Great Uncle Alex has some exciting stories to tell.

Why don't you talk to your nan about her childhood in Jamaica?

What questions to ask?

Once you've chosen the people you'd like to talk to, you'll need to think about what to ask.

This book has lots of questions for you to ask your grown-ups. It may also give you ideas for some questions of your own.

My action plan:

You can use this pad to help you get started.

People to talk to	Questions to ask
Grandpa Jacob	How did you meet Grandma?
Nana Cecile	Did you play any sports as a child?

Making plans

Once you feel happy with your questions, you'll need to fix a time to talk to your family members.

Talking to your grown-ups

If they live nearby, you could visit them at home.

If they are far away, you could make a video call.

Or sometimes you might decide that it's best to write a letter.

Keeping a record

You may like to write down your grown-ups' answers, but it's much easier to record your conversations. If you create an audio or video clip, you'll be able to play it back whenever you like. It may even become a valuable family record.

One day I may be showing this video to MY children!

Don't forget to double-check that the recording function is on.

A never-ending story

Finding out about your grown-ups' past doesn't have to end after just one conversation. Once your family start talking about their stories, they'll probably think of lots more things they'd like to share with you.

Are you ready to find out more about your family history?

Use this page to write down any more ideas, thoughts, or questions you have about your family history.

First memories and growing up

What do your grown-ups remember about their childhood?

This section will help to prompt memories of your grown-ups' childhoods, their time at school and their teenage years. And you'll probably hear some funny stories too!

First memories

Can you picture your grown-ups as babies and toddlers? Ask them what they remember about their early years.

Use this space for a photo or drawing.

You could ask...

What's the first thing you remember?

Who did you play with?

What kind of clothes did you wear?

My nana wore frilly romper suits.

Funny sayings

Did your grown-ups say funny things when they were young? Write them down here.

Early toys

Many adults remember a doll or teddy that they had when they were small. Maybe someone in your family still has a much-loved toy?

Some questions:

- What was your favourite soft toy when you were little?
- Did you have a doll's house, a play farm or a zoo?

In the 1960s, some children had pull-along toys like this.

Great Granny Lucy has kept this doll for over 80 years!

Toy story

You could write a story about a family toy and its adventures. Ask your grown-ups for ideas to help you.

Toys on the move

Some toys have changed a lot over the years. Ask your family about the kind of toy vehicles they used to play with.

Space toys were very popular in the 1960s.

You could ask...

- Did you collect toy cars?
- Did you play with a train set?
- Did you have a remote-controlled vehicle?

My Great Uncle Peter still has his toy car collection.

This clockwork train dates from the 1940s.

Games and puzzles

What kind of games did children play in the past? Were they very different from the games you play today?

Does anyone in your family know how to play 'Jacks'?

Some questions:

- What board games did you play?
- Did you play any computer games?
- Were you good at card games? Who did you play with?

These cards come from a vintage game of 'Happy Families'.

Let's play!

Ask one of your grown-ups to teach you a game they enjoyed when they were young. Maybe you will teach it to the next generation?

Name of the game:

Who taught you?

Was it fun?

Outdoor play

Children used to spend a lot of time outside, without any adults around. Ask your grown-ups about their memories of outdoor games.

You could ask...

- Where did you go to play outdoors?
- What kinds of games did you play?
- Did you ever build a den?

In the 1970s, children loved to bounce around on space hoppers.

"Can you come out to play?"

My half-sister loved climbing trees when she was little.

Whizzing around

Back in the 1950s, children had lots of interesting ways to get around. Which way looks most fun to you?

With your grown-up, rate them from 1 to 5.

Treasure hunting

Did your grown-ups ever search for treasure when they were young? You could draw a treasure map together.

Family pets

Pets can play an important part in a family's story. Ask about the animals your grown-ups remember.

Uncle Joey's pet rabbit, Mr Sniffles, once won a rosette.

In 1913, this man took his pet duck to a photographer's studio!

You could ask...

- Did you have any unusual family pets?
- Did your pet do funny things?

Great Grandpa trained his dog to fetch his slippers!

Pet portraits

Once you've found out about your family's pets, you can try drawing them. Don't forget to add their names and who they belonged to.

Memories of school

What was school like for your grown-ups? And were they good students – or not? You might be surprised by what you discover.

In the past, some children used a globe like this to learn about the countries of the world.

Learning

Which lessons did you enjoy? And which ones weren't much fun?

School rules

Did you ever break school rules? And did you end up in trouble?

Teachers

Were there some teachers you liked? And some who weren't so great?

School friends

Who were your best friends at school?

Great Uncle John loved to ask questions in class!

Memorable moments

What was the funniest/ silliest/scariest thing that happened to you at school?

Did your grown-ups ever use an ink pot and pen to write? Or maybe they had a cartridge or fountain pen.

Aunt Ro has a funny story about school dinners!

Sing out loud!

Did you have a school song? Can you sing it to me now?

More school memories

In Nana's school, a hand bell was rung at the end of each lesson.

School dinners

- Did you have school dinners and, if so, what were they like?

Special events and trips

- Do you remember school trips, plays or special events?

- Did they always go smoothly or were there some disasters?

School clothes

- Did you wear a uniform, and, if so, what was it like?

You could use this space for a photo or drawing of your grown-ups' school days.

With the help of your grown-up, compare school days in the past with school today. Think about school equipment, clothes, lessons and sports.

THEN...	AND NOW

When would you rather be a school pupil?

Teenage years

What kind of teenage trends were your family into? Were they the cool kids in their school? Some of their fashions look really funny now!

My step-mum loved her neon shellsuit in the 1990s.

You could ask...

- What was your biggest teenage adventure?
- Did you ever experiment with wacky clothes?
- What was your greatest fashion disaster?

How about hairstyles and make-up? Did your grown-ups try out any particular looks?

perm

Afro

beehive

pageboy

bowl cut

crew cut

mutton chops

mohawk

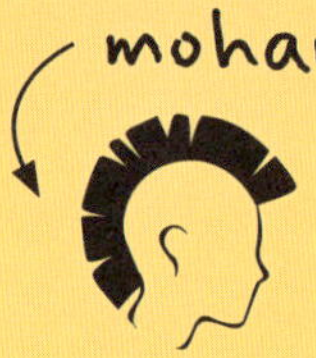

Teenage slang

Can your grown-ups remember some of their teenage slang? Write down words and phrases here.

"...dweeb, groovy, dude..."

Some questions:

- Which singers and bands did you follow?
- Did you go to pop concerts?
- Did you learn any special dances?

My gran loved going to music festivals!

Ask why you might need a pencil for this cassette.

Did your grown-ups have a record player, a boombox or maybe a walkman? And did they buy LPs, singles and cassettes?

Did you find out anything about your grown-ups' childhood which surprised you, or made you laugh? Make a note of it here.

Work, leisure and sport

What kind of work did your grown-ups do, and how did they spend their free time?

This section will help you learn about your grown-ups' working lives and their leisure activities. Maybe you'll find some sports and hobbies you can enjoy together.

Earning a living

Ask your grown-ups about their working lives. Was their work very different from jobs today?

People used to write letters on typewriters like this one.

Papa George was a mechanic. He even fixed racing cars!

You could ask...

- What was the best job you had? And the worst?

- Did you go to college before starting work?

- Do you have happy memories of your time at work?

Auntie Maureen was a chef.

My Great Grandma Bib was a nurse in the 1960s.

A day in a working life

Ask one of your grown-ups to tell you about their work routine.

Was your job very hard?

Did you wear special work clothes?

Did you make good friends at work?

What was the best part of your day?

Were there any low points?

How has the world of work changed over the last 50 years? Talk to an older person and note down your ideas.

THEN...	AND NOW

Earning pocket money

In the 1970s, many children had pocket-money jobs. Maybe one of your family worked in a shop or got up very early to deliver newspapers?

Growing things

Gardening skills are often passed down from one generation to the next. It's great to share the fun of growing things together.

We still use Great Aunt Devi's watering can.

You could ask...

- Who taught you about growing things?
- Did you grow some plants of your own when you were little?
- Were some harder to grow than others?

Make a mini family garden

Why not try creating a mini family garden in a plant pot or patch of earth? Ask a grown-up to help you fill it with family favourites.

Plants in our family garden	Reasons for planting

Grampy calls these flowers 'little grapes'.

Making things

Are there people in your family who like to sew or knit, or who enjoy woodwork or pottery? You could ask them to share their skills with you.

My oma taught me to crochet.

Some questions:

- When did you start making things?
- Who taught you your skills?
- What was the first thing you made?

Making things together

Try making something with a grown-up – you will be learning a family skill that you could pass on in the future.

I helped my Uncle Marek make a wooden nesting box.

Uncle Amir collects coins from all the countries he has visited.

Collecting things

Does one of your grown-ups have a special collection? How did they get started? And do they have suggestions for things you could collect?

You could ask...

- What was the first item in your collection?
- Were some items hard to find?
- How do you like to display your collection?

Start collecting!

Ask your family for some tips on starting your own collection.

1)

2)

3)

Poppa has been collecting rocks and minerals since he was a boy.

Making music

Music can play a big part in family life. Do you sometimes make music as a family? Or maybe you all sing along to some favourite tunes.

Uncle Leon is teaching me to play the saxophone.

Some questions:

- Do any pieces of music bring back special memories?
- Did you learn to play a musical instrument?
- Did you ever sing in a group or a choir?

BOOM, THUD

Nana Zuri plays the drums.

Let's make music!

Ask an older person to teach you a song they learned when they were young.

Playing sport

Were your grown-ups keen on sport when they were young? Maybe you share a passion for the same sport?

You could ask...

- What was your favourite sport?
- Were there some sports you didn't like?

HIT... OR MISS?

....'s greatest sporting triumph:

....'s greatest sporting disaster:

More questions:

- Did you take part in competitions?
- Did you do lots of training?
- Did you win any prizes?

How has sport changed over the years? Ask your family about the clothes they wore and the equipment they used.

THEN...	AND NOW

Show me some moves!

Some older people still practise their sporting skills. You could ask your grown-ups to demonstrate some memorable moves.

Auntie Trish taught dance aerobics in the 1980s.

...5...6...7...8!

Watching sport

Which sports do your grown-ups like to follow? And what got them started as supporters?

I go to football matches with my dads and my grandad. It's a family tradition!

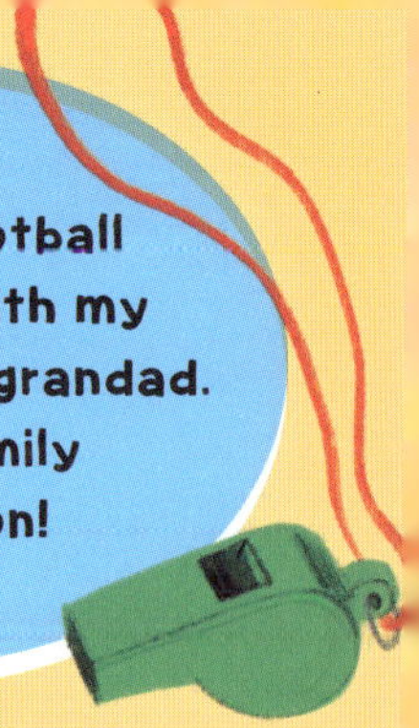

You could ask...

- What sports did you watch when you were growing up?
- Who were your sporting heroes?

Sporting heroes

Ask your grown-up to pick a sports star from the past to compare with one today. Then fill in this chart together.

THEN...	AND NOW
Name:	Name:
Sport:	Sport:
Special skills:	Special skills:
Greatest achievement:	Greatest achievement:

Allan Hopkins was an Australian Rules footballer in the Victorian Football League.

Loyal supporters

How involved did your grown-ups get in their favourite sport?

✓ Did anyone in your family:

- ◯ Wear a team scarf and colours?
- ◯ Own a football strip?
- ◯ Travel to watch matches, races or competitions?
- ◯ Collect sports stickers or cards?

Great Auntie Molly was a keen motor-racing fan.

Granny Betty introduced me to baseball. Now we follow it together.

SPORTS CHALLENGE

Does someone in your family follow a sport you've never watched before? You could try watching it together and they could explain the rules and what to look out for.

Family entertainment

Which books and magazines did your grown-ups enjoy when they were young? And which TV shows and films do they still remember?

You could ask...

- Which characters did you like in books and on TV?
- Did you have a weekly magazine or comic?

What a show!

Did your grown-ups go to:

- ○ The cinema
- ○ The theatre
- ○ A circus
- ○ A ballet
- ○ A pantomime?

✓ Add a tick

Grandpa Tim was really into space adventures.

Movie review

Watch an old film with one of your grown-ups. Then write a review together. You'll probably find you've noticed very different things.

Name of the film:

Year that it was released:

Our score:

___ / 10

Good points:

Bad points:

What makes it different from a modern film:

Much-loved books

Does someone in your family love to read? Ask them to suggest three books they think you'd enjoy.

My Aunt Daisy has kept all her books about pony riding.

....'s book list:

1)

2)

3)

Whose talents or hobbies would you like to know more about? You could use this page for some notes.

Life at home

What can your grown-ups tell you about the places where they lived and their life at home?

This section covers memories of your grown-ups' childhood homes. You'll find pages on family meals and celebrations, and some great ideas for sharing family recipes.

Family homes

Do your grown-ups have memories of where they grew up? Try talking to your family about important places from their childhood.

Poppa's childhood bedroom had painted stars on the ceiling.

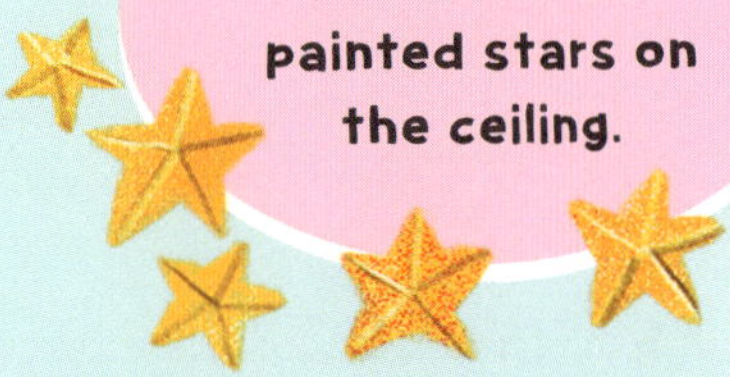

You could ask...

- What do you remember about a childhood home?
- Can you describe some:
  - wallpaper
  - furniture
  - ornaments?

Sometimes a comfy old chair will stay in a family home for years.

If you have some photos, you could stick them here.

Do you remember?

Ask a grown-up to help you draw a picture of a home that they remember.

Seeing Granny's childhood home felt like stepping into the past.

Auntie Rosa grew up in a tiny Spanish village.

My grandad's family lived on the 17th floor of a tower block.

Visiting the past

Your grown-ups may be able to show you a home where they once lived.

Moving home

Granny remembers moving across the country in the 1950s.

Not all families stay in one place. Your grown-ups may have memories of moving home and sometimes even settling in a different country.*

*There's more about moving countries on page 73.

Moving memories

How old were you when you moved home?

Where was your old home?

Where was your new home?

Was it a long journey?

How did you feel about moving?

Can you remember the first day in your new home?

Sometimes a special item, such as a clock, is passed on by each generation.

Pieces of home

Ask your grown-ups if they have kept something special to remind them of a childhood home. You could draw a picture of it and tell its story.

Auntie Kay's hula dancer stood on her bedside table.

This lamp was in my grampy's house when he was growing up.

Family meals

Most people have vivid memories of meals they loved – or hated! Ask your grown-ups what meals stand out for them.

Auntie Pia makes the BEST pasta dishes!

You could ask...

- Which foods did you love?
- Did you help with the cooking?
- Did you have any cooking disasters?

Special foods

What special treats do your grown-ups remember?

Parties	Christmas and Celebrations	Picnics and BBQs

'Family Favourites' feast

What would YOUR family choose?

Super Starters

You could add some photos.

Amazing Mains

Delicious Desserts

Family recipes

Is there a family recipe that you could learn to cook? Try it out first, then use these pages to write it down.

Recipe name:

Ingredients:

Method:

Our family recipe book has been handed down for three generations.

Make a family recipe book

You could collect some family favourites to pass on to the next generation. Ask different people in your family to write down a recipe they love.

Celebrations

When people look back on the past, certain days stand out. Ask your grown-ups if they remember some special occasions, such as birthdays and Christmas, religious festivals and family weddings.

My aunties still talk about their parties in the 1970s.

You could ask...

- Did you dress up in special clothes?
- Did you decorate your house?
- Did you sing any songs?

The PERFECT present

Can your grown-ups remember a best-ever gift? And do they know what happened to it?

Party games

Ask someone in your family to describe a party game they used to play. Do you think it sounds fun?

Name of the game:

How to play:

Fun-factor rating: ___/10

Love and romance

Do your grown-ups remember their first girlfriend or boyfriend? And what about their first date? It can be fun to find out about your family's romantic moments.

Fill this page with stories about YOUR family home. Does it hold any special memories for you?

Travel and holidays

How did your grown-ups get around, and do they remember some special journeys and holidays?

This section covers the different kinds of transport your grown-ups may have used. You'll also find pages on holidays and longer family journeys.

Getting around

How did your grown-ups get around when they were young? Did their family own a car? Did they travel by bus or train?

This school bus dates from the 1950s.

Gramps took the tram to school every morning.

You could ask...

- How did you get to school?
- What type of transport did you use most often?
- Did you have a bicycle?

✓ Did anyone in your family own a:

- ○ motorbike
- ○ campervan
- ○ truck
- ○ boat?

My first wheels

Ask a family member to help you fill in this chart all about the first vehicle they owned.

Make and model:

Colour:

Nickname:

Top speed:

Easy to drive?

Did it ever break down?

How long did you keep it?

Can you remember any special journeys?

Family journeys

What kind of journeys did your grown-ups take when they were young? Some of them may have memories of fun trips and outings. Others may have taken long and difficult journeys.

How did you travel?

Circle the form of transport.

plane ferry car
train coach
ocean liner other

Journeys to remember

Ask your grown-up to help you complete these travel memories.

Where did you leave from?

Where did you travel to?

Who did you go with?

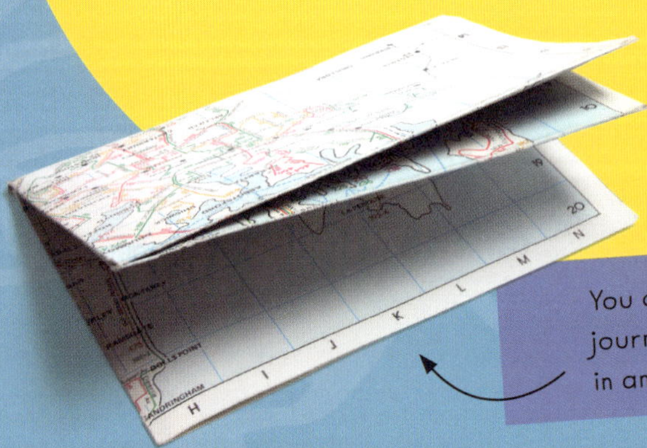

You could follow the journey on a map or in an atlas.

What did you see and do?

How long did the journey take?

Leaving for good

Some families travel to a different country to start a new kind of life. Has anyone in your family moved to a new country?

Fill this ticket with details of your family's BEST EVER day trip.

MY MOST MEMORABLE DAY TRIP

WHEN:

WHERE:

WHAT MADE IT SO SPECIAL:

Family holidays

Auntie Mei loved going to the beach.

Many people have happy memories of going on holiday. Talk to your family about holidays they loved – and some trips that went wrong!

Where did you go?

What sights did you see?

What was the best part of the holiday?

In the 1970s, caravans and campervans were very popular.

Holiday postcards

You could add a photo or a drawing to your card.

Ask your grown-ups to help you fill in these postcards with their memories, good and bad!

- Did anything go wrong on a family holiday? And did it work out all right in the end?

My foster dad got stung by a jellyfish!

Holiday disaster!

Our holiday treats

- Maybe your family enjoyed some special holiday meals?

Holiday souvenirs

Ask your family if they kept any souvenirs to remind them of their holiday. Or perhaps they have some photos to show you?

Would you like to have gone on any of the journeys you've found out about? Why, or why not?

Living through history

How does your family story fit into the wider history of the world?

Use these pages to help uncover memories of major news events, and to explore the changes your grown-ups have seen. There's also advice on how to research the more distant past.

IN THE NEWS

Most people remember some major news events from when they were young. Are there some special moments that your grown-ups have never forgotten?

What stood out for you?

Ask a family member to list their top three newsworthy events. What made them choose those three?

1)

2)

3)

WHOOSH

Your grown-ups may have witnessed a world-first event.

My Great Auntie Joanna watched the first moon landing on TV.

My grandad saw The Beatles playing their first concert!

Did someone in your family take part in an event that later became famous?

Some of your family will remember an important person's wedding or funeral.

My nana was in the crowd at a royal wedding.

YAY!

HOORAY!

FIND OUT MORE...

What other big events took place while your grown-ups were young? Ask them to help you find some books in the library or look up events online. You may be able to watch some video clips together.

Use this space to write down what you found.

Changing times

People in your family will have lived through many changes. Ask them about the differences between their childhood and the way we live now.

You could ask...

How have cars changed since you were young?

What about computers?

How has day-to-day shopping changed?

Everyday items go through many changes as technology advances. With the help of your grown-up, draw or find a picture of...

THEN...	AND NOW
A telephone	
A television	
A music system	

Can you find out what this is?

Forgotten words

What do you think these things are? Ask some older family members to explain them.

mangle

wireless

clotheshorse

teasmade

gramophone

8-track

Can you think of some more old-fashioned words to add?

BRRM BRMMM

This Cadillac dates from the 1950s. Did anyone in your family get to ride in a car like this?

Looking back

Some of your older grown-ups will have stories to tell of family members from past generations. These memories are a precious reminder of people who lived a long time ago.

Who were your great-great grandparents? And what can you find out about them?

You could ask...

- How far back can we trace our family?
- Can you tell me some family names?

Family places

Try to discover where your family once lived. Maybe you could visit a place that your ancestors came from?

This is the street where my great-great granny was born.

Cornwall, England, 1900

Family research

It's possible to learn a lot about family history by researching old records of births, marriages and deaths. Today, many records like these can be found online.

Are there any news events from the past that you would like to have witnessed?

Telling your family story

How can you present your family history?

Look through the next few pages for exciting ways to tell your family story. You'll find ideas for scrapbooks, collages and videos, and a guide to creating your own family tree.

Family story ideas

This book could be the starting point for many exciting projects. Here are just a few ways to present your family history.

I've designed a collage in the shape of a family tree.*

Try creating a collage from family photos.

*For more on family trees, turn to page 90.

Fill a scrapbook with postcards, tickets and photos.

Mount some family photos on cards and hang them from branches.

We think this makes a great decoration!

Arrange some treasured items on a 'family memory shelf'.

I've made a display of objects with special memories.

Aunt Jenny's collection of snowglobes from her travels.

Grandma's teddy 'Boris' from 1952.

Great Grandad's camera that he always took on holiday.

Make a memory jar

You could fill a jar with written memories waiting to be opened sometime in the future.

* Ask your family members to write down a special memory to put in the jar.
* Make a plan for when you would like to open the jar.

We're keeping our memory jar to pass on to future generations.

More ideas

Here are some more ideas to bring your family story to life.

You could produce an audio-visual library with recordings from different people in your family.

We recorded our family telling stories and singing songs.

Now we can listen to Aunt Izzy's funny stories whenever we want.

You could create a family map, showing where people live and some journeys they have made.

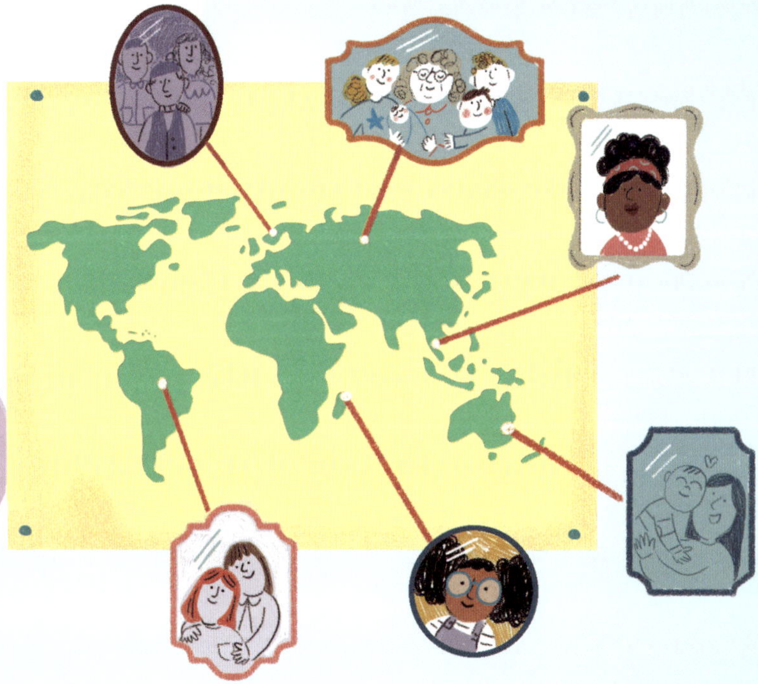

My grandparents travelled across the world to start a new life.

Some families piece together a patchwork memory quilt. Its squares are made from shirts, dresses and baby clothes once worn by the family.

Even more things to do

* Put together a family joke book. Ask each of your family members to contribute a joke.

* Put on a play showing some scenes from your family history.

* Write a postcard to someone in your family who lived long ago.

Maybe you can add some activities of your own?

Family trees

Creating a family tree is a very good way to show how your family fits together. Here are two different kinds of 'trees'.

This diagram is called a 'family tree' because it has lots of branches, even though it doesn't look like a tree!

1) You may like to create a diagram like this.

You could decide to show just part of your family to keep it simple.

2) Many families don't fit neatly into a diagram like the one above. Instead, you could create a tree like this and write the names of your special people on its leaves.

Make your own family tree

Use this page to create your own family tree. Choose which kind of tree you'd like to show and add your family names. You could ask your grown-ups to help you.

If you have a big family, you may need a very large piece of paper!

Ruby Dover

(Grandma)

Write family names as well as their relationship to you on the 'tree'.

Ruby Dover

(Grandma)
b. 1948

You could also add dates of birth, if you know them.

b. = born

My notes and pictures

You can use this space for more stories, photos and drawings. Maybe you have some memories of your own that you'd like to note down here?

Family history words

Here are some explanations of the family words used in this book.

adoptive parent a parent who was chosen to look after you because your birth parents weren't able to

ancestor a member of your family who lived a long time ago

aunt the sister of one of your parents, or the wife or partner of your uncle or aunt

birth parents the parents you had when you were born

cousin a child of your aunt or uncle

family tree a picture showing how people in a family are connected to each other

foster parent a parent who looks after you for a while if your birth parents aren't able to

generation a name for all the people born around the same time. Families are made up of several generations.

grandfather the father of one of your parents

grandmother the mother of one of your parents

great aunt the aunt of one of your parents

great grandparent the grandparent of one of your parents

great uncle the uncle of one of your parents

half-sibling someone who shares one birth parent with you

parent a mum or dad

relative someone who is related to you or one of your parents

sibling a brother or sister

step-sibling a child of your step-parent

step-parent someone who is married to one of your parents

uncle the brother of one of your parents, or the husband or partner of your aunt or uncle

My family words

What words do your family members use for each other? You can write them down here.

Acknowledgements

Every effort has been made to trace and acknowledge ownership of copyright. If any rights have been omitted, the publishers offer to rectify this in any subsequent editions following notification. The publishers are grateful to the following organizations and individuals for their contributions and permission to reproduce copyright material:

p19 (top right) Shotshop GmbH/Alamy Stock Photo; p20 (top left) ClassicStock/Alamy Stock Photo; p20 (top middle) Werner Otto/Alamy Stock Photo; p20 (top right) Paul Pickford/Alamy Stock Photo; p20 (bottom left) Kirn Vintage Stock/Alamy Stock Photo; p20 (bottom middle) Classic Picture Library/Alamy Stock Photo; p21 (top right) Michaela Stejskalova/Alamy Stock Photo; p28 (top left) ClassicStock/Alamy Stock Photo; p29 (middle right) Some Wonderful Old Things/Alamy Stock Photo; p29 (bottom left) Vintage Image/ Alamy Stock Photo; p29 (bottom right) Robyn Mackenzie/Alamy Stock Photo; p30 (middle left) Marc Tielemans/Alamy Stock Photo; p30 (bottom right) pictureline/Alamy Stock Photo; p31 (middle right) Andrew Gardner/Alamy Stock Photo; p32 (bottom left) Heritage Image Partnership Ltd/Alamy Stock Photo; p34 (top right) Prestor Pictures LLC/Alamy Stock Photo; p35 (top right) Classic Picture Library/ Alamy Stock Photo; p36 (top right) incamerastock/Alamy Stock Photo; p36 (bottom left) Ewing Galloway/Alamy Stock Photo; p38 (top right) Elisabeth Burrell/Alamy Stock Photo; p40 (bottom left) Frank Chmura/Alamy Stock Photo; p44 (top right) Anuparp Adisai/ Alamy Stock Photo; p45 (top middle) Tony Henshaw/Alamy Stock Photo; p46 (bottom left) Lee Avison/Alamy Stock Photo; p47 (top right) deefish/Alamy Stock Photo; p47 (bottom middle) Opas Chotiphantawanon/Alamy Stock Photo; p48 (top left) Sergio Delle Vedove/ Alamy Stock Photo; p48 (bottom) Andriana Syvanych/Alamy Stock Photo; p49 (bottom left) Ray A. Akey/Alamy Stock Photo; p49 (bottom middle) Gino's Premium Images/Alamy Stock Photo; p51 (top left) Houndstooth Archive/Alamy Stock Photo; p51 (bottom left) Ewing Galloway/Alamy Stock Photo; p52 (bottom left) History and Art Collection/Alamy Stock Photo; p59 (bottom right) dbphots/ Alamy Stock Photo; p61 (top left) Nikreates/Alamy Stock Photo; p61 (bottom right) Ivan Smuk/Alamy Stock Photo; p64 (bottom left) Picture Partners/Alamy Stock Photo; p65 (top left) Ian Shaw/Alamy Stock Photo; p66 (top right) ClassicStock/Alamy Stock Photo; p67 (bottom left) Ewing Galloway/Alamy Stock Photo; p70 (top left) canbedone/Alamy Stock Photo; p72 (bottom left) Digifoto Sapphire/ Alamy Stock Photo; p74 (bottom right) Justin Kase zsixz/Alamy Stock Photo; p80 (bottom left) Ian Dagnall/Alamy Stock Photo; p81 (bottom left) Kevin Britland/Alamy Stock Photo; p82 (top right) Chronicle/Alamy Stock Photo; p82 (bottom right) Niday Picture Library/Alamy Stock Photo; p83 (bottom left) Universal Images Group North America LLC/Alamy Stock Photo; p83 (bottom middle) 914 collection/Alamy Stock Photo

With special thanks to Jane Bingham and Max Jeffries for use of their family photos.

Additional editing by Alice Beecham. Additional illustrations by Irena Freitas.
Additional design by Matt Durber. Additional advice from Katie White.

First published in 2026 by Usborne Publishing Limited, 83-85 Saffron Hill, London EC1N 8RT, United Kingdom. usborne.com